Brazos View

BRAZOS HOUSE

Brazos View

Charles Inge

Temple, Texas

ISBN 978-0-9824405-1-3
Library of Congress Control Number: 2010932910
Manufactured in the United States of America

Front Cover Drawing, Frontispiece,
and End Drawing by
Virginia Erickson

Ink Brush Press
Temple, Texas
www.inkbrushpress.com

The Brazos View poems

are dedicated to Dominique—

loving wife, friend, co-worker,

confidante, and partner

for twenty-eight years,

September 4th, this year.

Only our being together

makes Brazos View.

Acknowledgements

Beginning in the fall of 2004, annual four-day presentations at the Dora Lee Langdon Cultural & Educational Center here in Granbury, sponsored by Tarleton State University (Stephenville), have brought an array of creative talent from various fields of artistic expression—fiction and non-fiction, poetry, painting, printmaking, photography, cinema, plays, music, and dance—to our North Texas community. These conferences, usually referred to as Tarleton's Langdon Weekends, provide a venue for attendees to read, perform, teach, critique, and preview current work. Many of the resulting artistic efforts are submitted for publication in an accompanying annual anthology, *The Langdon Review of the Arts in Texas*, published by Tarleton State University.

The stimulation of these weekend workshops refocused my lifelong interest in poetry, and resulted in the first group of *Brazos View* poems. Ten of these poems appeared in Volume 3 of the *Langdon Review,* and I wish to acknowledge with special gratitude Volume 3 co-editors Marilyn Robitaille and Donna Walker-Nixon. The *Brazos View* collection now contains 140 poems, from which 115 have been selected for this Ink Brush Press publication.

The encouragement, recognition, and inspiration received from some of the outstanding poets attending the Langdon Weekend conferences manifests now in publication of this recently expanded version of *Brazos View*—Alan Birkelbach, Jerry Bradley, Jerry Craven, Sherry Craven, Jeffrey DeLotto, James Hoggard, Karla Morton, Frances Neidhardt, Naomi Shihab Nye, and Larry Thomas, among others. My thanks to each of you—and to Tarleton State University for sponsoring events and publications of such widespread significance and influence.

The Ink Brush Press crew—Press Director Jerry Craven, Editor-in-Chief Carroll Wilson, Editor Sherry Craven, and Art Editor Lisa Craig have been supportive and encouraging throughout the publishing process, and their encouragement and assistance are much appreciated.

Versions of some of the pieces in *Brazos View* have appeared previously:

"Two Chairs," "Angularities (At Dawn)," *Amarillo Bay*™ *Literary Magazine* (www.amarillobay.org) ,(Volume 11, Number 1, February 2009.

"Eupatorium," "Brazos Pathing," "An Upper Room," "Cetacean," "The Lake at Night," "Wind Patterns," Cormorant," "A Winter Morning," *Langdon Review of the Arts in Texas , Vol. 3, 2006-2007,* (Stephenville, TX: Tarleton State University).

"The Moth" (retitled "Realms"), *4th Annual Chips Off the Writers Bloc* (Granbury, TX: The Writers Bloc, 2005).

"Sea Seine," *3rd Annual Chips Off the Writers Bloc* (Granbury, TX: The Writers Bloc, 2004).

"The 4th," *Granbury Showcase Magazine,* July/August 2005, Granbury, Texas.

CONTENTS

Illustrations

Preface

Almost a decade after Dominique and I met and married, we purchased the first of the three properties that now comprise our Brazos House homeplace. It consisted of a small stone cottage with an adjoining lot, which we bought originally as a weekend getaway. Our second piece, fronting along the lake, lay west of a portion of that original lot, creating an L-shaped property. The third purchase filled in the L-shape so that today the Brazos House land is roughly rectangular, containing in area a bit less than two acres, with 450 feet of frontage on Lake Granbury in Hood County, Texas.

Our coming here was rather roundabout. In travels we had taken during our first years together, a number of the places we visited had been considered as locations we might want to move to in future years. I was by then beginning the winding down of my business interests. The home we occupied in Dallas, although charming, was quite small. And it was an older house, which had been remodeled a couple of times. We both loved it but finally concluded we eventually would move, and that when we did so it would be somewhere away from the tempo and traffic of Dallas, my boyhood home.

Dominique's childhood had been spent primarily in Atlanta so we seriously considered going to the Georgia coast where her parents then lived. As late as five years after buying our lakeside weekend getaway we were still contemplating more remote locations for a permanent home. Yet we had become attached to our little cottage on Lake Granbury, and finally decided to sell the Dallas property and build a new residence on the adjoining open land here.

The decision to custom-build a home rather than to buy one already built was a difficult decision to make. Between us we had had enough experience with building and remodeling to know what lay ahead. Moreover, we knew the process of constructing a new home would seriously disrupt the property we had just spent eight years improving.

The collection of vignettes in *Brazos View* does not deal with the trials and tribulations experienced during construction of the substantial residence we built here. The dust, dirt, delays, false starts, cost overruns and contractual entanglements attendant to the activity of building a custom home seemed unsuited to being recorded in poetic form. Yet the building project was a creative one, with the final product particularly gratifying after the long struggle for its realization.

We were, overall, five years in this process—three years in the planning, and two years building. During the building phase the whole property suffered from disruptions as well as some neglect; to such an extent that it took several years following this work to get our grounds back to the condition we had earlier achieved.

Throughout the construction of the larger house we lived in the weekend cottage, immediately next door. That proved quite helpful in supervising the work, though it did result in an unimaginable number of early morning calls. This building project was completed now more than ten years ago.

We named the house and property Brazos House for its location at the end of Brazos Street. And for its site on a bluff above the lake formed from the damming of the Brazos River, in the late 1960s. This property and the lake, with its river, became the locus for our *views*—hence the title for this collection of poems, *Brazos View*.

First and foremost, poetry is about focus: usually focus on thoughts, feelings, persons, places, or events. These vignettes focus variously, but concentrate mostly on this place, attempting to evoke how it was, how it is today, its aspects and dimensions, its often transformative effect on our lives. Our place here, like many others perhaps, truly was, and is, an undiscovered world. Do we ever really see or know beyond the least little bit of what there is to be seen and known, anywhere?

Welcome to *Brazos View*. I hope you find here some of the same richness and enjoyment that we who live here do, each and every day.

Spring, 2010
Charles Inge
Brazos House
Granbury, Texas

Memorable Firsts

Brazos View

This bluffside site
  overlooking
a river dammed to
  form a narrow
winding lake, thirty-
  five miles north
to south; at
  midpoint of the lake
as the lake itself is
  near midpoint
of the river's
  circuitous course,
extending from its
  sources near the
Texas-New Mexico border
  down to the Gulf.
As much as
  anything else,
it was the bouldered
  bluff and
mirroring lake,
  with the promise
of unending skyscapes
  overhead—and
the many birds
  active here—
that brought us
  to Brazos View.

The Little House

It seemed
  too perfect—
the right place
  at the right time,
an hour-and-a-half
  from home
yet, *light years away.*
  A small property
in a small town—
  perched at (and beyond)
the brink
  of a rocky bluff,
overlooking a lake;
  an architect's dream.

Two levels, dug
  right into the rock,
hand-cut stone
  with metal roof,
cedar-planked within.
  Upstairs, a cathedral ceiling
and large box-bay
  opened this room
to its view
  (with a clever built-in
kitchen across one wall).
  The downstairs room,
opened onto a sun deck
  extending over the lake.

A wonder of compactness
  and efficiency,
basically two rooms—
  the upper for dining
and daily living, with
  sleeping room below
(bathroom on each level,
  and fireplaces, too).
One block off of
  the little town's square,
yet private, secluded,
  an enclosed courtyard
before, and lake behind—
  just what we'd hoped to find.

A circular iron stair
  from the deck
to the ground,
  then a short set
of steps to lakeshore,
  where the boathouse
was found—
  normally not given
to hurried decisions,
  in this case it took
Dominique and me
  a bit less
than an hour
  to make up our minds.

The Halcyon Bird

Long known in
   fable and myth,
daughter of a king,
   lost at sea,
to reemerge—
   Alcyone.
The first bird
   of our first
day at Brazos View.

Not that we
   believed in
omens, but
   fair winds,
a calm sea,
   happiness
and prosperity,
   ought not
be declined.

The Romans
   called the
kingfisher, Halcyon
   (as it's known
today), a bird
   in its various
forms found almost
   round the world:
the Halcyon bird.

Standing on
   the back deck
of the stone cottage,
   on a Monday
afternoon, we
   saw it dive,
plunge into the lake and
   reemerge with a silver
shad shining in its beak.

Odd; the bird,
   and our being there
so close to home
   looking at a place
to live ... *just
   weekends*, we said, *a
perfect weekend getaway.*
   And for a decade
it would stay that way.

Unquestionably
   the little house
was a gem,
   well-designed and
sturdily built of stone,
   with a copper roof;
anchored in the rocks
   of a bluff
overlooking the lake.

After the Purchase

It was quite early
  in the year,
after our purchase closed,
  the first weekend we
had a chance to go down
  the weather turned bad
and everything froze.
  With roadways impassable,
we sat home and fumed:
  was the heat on;
would the pipes freeze;
  was the place secure;
who did we know
  to call?

Turned out winter here
  is very nearly the best
season of the year—
  snug in that dramatic
upstairs room with its
  view out over the lake,
fireplace warm and bright,
  Dominique about the magic
of our evening meal,
  or reading, or playing
some board game with me,
  together hoping for one
of those fiery sunset skies
  seen often in wintertime.

Our initial purchase
  included a large
adjacent lot with
  several nice trees,
though its soil was thin
  and vegetation ragged;
we knew the coming
  spring might prove
challenging, transforming
  cockleburs and grass burrs
into gardens and lawn.
  Beyond its westmost lines,
lay an abandoned house
  and a church parking lot.

Challenging indeed—
  tools first, of course,
lawn mower, shovels, rakes
  wheelbarrow, hoses and
garden tools—then a
  shed to store it all in,
and fencing to make secure
  (white stone columns with
cedar slatting in between).
  Plus this bit of folly,
added in; one *deluxe, green*
  and white striped double
hammock, which went unused
  for several years.

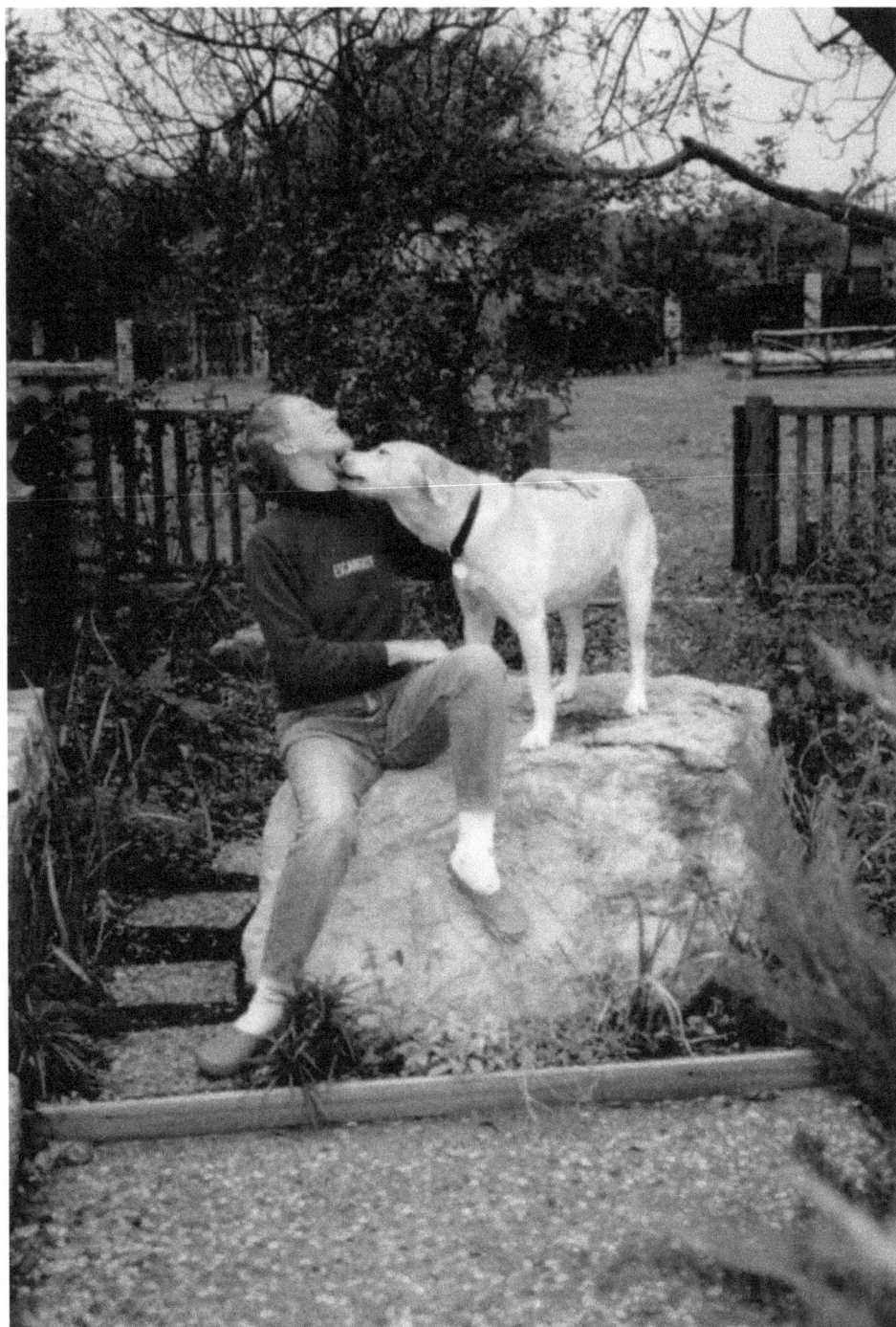

Dominique and Brindle

The Next Big Step

Within a year
  of our first purchase
the lakefront property
  immediately west
came up for sale.
  Much neglected and
overpriced—we thought
we would *wait a while.*

Yet, abandoned several
  years, it was such
an eyesore—the house
  a wreck, two
rusty metal sheds, the yard
  a dumping ground.
Screen planting, possibly, or
  trompe l'oeils, for the sheds.

Trompe l'oeils—Dominique's
  suggestion for improving
the appearance of whatever's
  unattractive to the eye—
would, of course,
  require owner's approval.
Probably not a good idea;
  let's see what happens.

When the price
  did come down
we moved quickly—
  thus doubling the size
of our *getaway place,*
  and more than
doubling the work.
  Now what?

A bulldozer and
  two dump trucks
made quick work of
  the dilapidated structures
and accumulated debris.
  For us, it was like
watching a flower unfold, the
  property's beauty revealed.

Trees, elevation,
  views, the lake—
a wonderful palette.
  Lawn in the foreyard space,
around the large live oak tree;
  a garden *here*, flowers
there, *a stone terrace* at
  the chimney we had saved.

Picking Up

Square-head
   handmade
nails, bottles
   broken and
unbroken, rusted
   horseshoes and
hinges, cast-off
   tools, bed springs,
old tires, barbed
   wire, tin cans
and abandoned auto
   body parts—
for many
   years (before
the lake was in)
   the bluff at
Brazos View
   must have been
someone's backyard
   dumping ground . . .
making for us
   a most interesting job
of picking up
   what was left
lying around.

Building the Bridge

Red-Letter Days

As soon as cleanup
   on the new lot was done,
improvements were begun:
   lawn, a decorative
perimeter fence, stone
   terrace at the chimney,
and a large garden plot
   enclosed with cedar rails.

At south end of the terrace,
   the old chimney recapped
was then strengthened by
   an extension of the hearth;
at north end a trellis of
   cedar posts was constructed
(for roses), which Dominique
   dubbed, *the pergola*.

By their nature cedar
   structures are rough-hewn
but the care taken
   in planning and design of
the trellis and garden rails
   suggested we might use
those same workmen to put up
   a good potting shed.

Grading for an entrance drive
   uncovered a long abandoned
water well, which we at once
   decided to revive. . . .
Men were hired to clear the
   hillside above the lake,
so overgrown and trashed
   it seemed impenetrable.

Lawn, garden and roses
   now beginning to grow,
Big Jim, Danny, Serafin and
   John, finished and gone,
weekends were too short to
   get all our work done—
an ad was composed: *Organic*
   gardener needed, 2 days/wk.

Mike answered that ad.
   He was *handy at almost*
anything, and he knew about
   organics. By summer's end
the place looked lovely, and
   Mike and I, in August heat,
had made a lakeside trail, plus
   a forty-foot wooden bridge

Going Organic

—first, test the soil—

It would take
   three years to
achieve the right balance.
   The mineral nutrients
in our soil were
   locked up, amendments
needed to be applied;
   fish emulsion, molasses
and humate at the garden,
   alfalfa meal drench and
foliar spray for the roses.

Only natural pest controls—
   diatomaceous earth,
pyrethrum, rotenone;
   ladybugs, lacewings
and other beneficial insects
   were brought in.
Slowly the garden soil became
   rich and friable enough
for vigorous, healthy plants.
   Organic fertilizers and
aerating fixed the lawn.

Steps

The layers
   of limestone
in our bluffside
   blocks
tend over time
   to weather
away . . . and should
   be easy
 to cut.

I wanted
   steps in
the natural rock,
   and setting about
to cut a few,
   with rock hammer
and chisels
   began
to chip away.

The boulders
   gave back
better than
   they got,
the chisels just
   danced around . . .
three days' work made
   three small steps,
and that was that.

I and We

Isn't it true,
  almost anytime
there is a big job
  to do, it involves
someone else, too?

At Brazos View,
  I or we
means Dominique,
  Mike or me, or any
combination of us three.

Dominique knows the
  plants: which zones,
sun or shade, alkaline or
  acid, and even those
impossible taxonomic names.

She gets the catalogs—
  seeds, plants, bulbs,
tools, all the gear to
  do the work; and
she schedules everything.

Mike now has eighteen
  years of notebooks filled
with schedules, projects
  and chores: he is
essential to Brazos View.

Mike knows his bugs:
  which are harmful,
which beneficial, and
  their habits; thus
how to gain control.

I just know a
  little bit about
a lot of things—
  sometimes a help,
sometimes a hindrance.

Trees, rocks, birds and
  grass are my forte,
common sense my
  best defense, and a
special talent for minutia.

Spring's First Call

This morning
  we heard
the redbird's
  clear
repetitive call
  announcing
spring is here.
  Soon nest building
will begin—
  mockingbirds,
robins, wrens.

Brazos View
  will have a role
to play in nest
  preparation activity—
cleaning and remounting
  (on tall, metal poles)
our several martin houses,
  down by the lake—
then we'll watch and
  wait, as renewal of
another year begins.

Martins

Swallows are everywhere in good repute
—T. Gilbert Pearson

Our first
  purple martins
arrived at
  Brazos View
on Valentine's Day
  this year,
their houses having
  just gone up
the day before.
  One of the season's
special events
  was now
about to begin.

These scouts first,
  three black specks
against the sky,
  checking the
lay of the land;
  two ounces each
of feather, fluff and
  avian bone,
at end of a
  four thousand
mile run—
  their cohorts
some days behind.

Among the most
  gregarious of
birds, martins
  fly in loose-knit
flocks and nest
  in multiple pairs;
and are welcomed
  on their return each
year for their
  cheery calls,
aerobatics, and all
  the pesky insects
they consume.

As box selection, bonding,
  and nest building
begin . . . twigs, grass
  and leaves are
stuffed and woven
  into nesting pads;
then, the laying and
  brooding of eggs,
and care and feeding
  of hatchlings, until
they fledge—too soon, the
  lure of their southern skies
will call them home again.

Vagaries

Yesterday,
   Brazos View
was caught up
   in the full onslaught
of spring, the weather
   unseasonably warm,
birds clamoring, trees
   and flowers rushing
pell-mell into bloom.

Today
   it snowed,
and Brazos View became
   a softly muffled place,
its rash of reds, yellows,
   pinks and blues,
all a powdery white;
   now the weather news
predicts a freeze tonight.

Stone Staircase, Lake and Bluff

Blue Heron

Its primordial
   a-a-wk,
calling back
   across eons
to the earliest times
   of the great
seas that
   left as residue
this bluffside
   fishing place.

At that time
   when large
and awkward
   seemed
evolution's fate,
   the beauty
of beasts
   taking first flight
must have been
   an awesome sight.

Patient, patient
   at fishing
tasks . . . an
   eccentric, one-legged
dignitary atop the
   martins' house . . .
effortlessly
   graceful in
gliding
   flight.

Four feet long and
   a six-foot
span, passing
   elegantly
by our lakeside
   bluff . . .
a creature worthy
   of taking
an ancient world's
   breath away.

Danny and Big Jim

Great excitement
  at Brazos View—
the building kit
  for Dominique's
potting shed arrived.

A site had been
  selected near
the west garden plot,
  a sunny,
south-facing spot.

Eight feet
  by twelve
(and eight feet tall),
  we would need
some help after all.

We had employed
  Big Jim before,
and liked his work;
  a date was picked
to begin.

Danny was Big Jim's
  helper—they had
worked together awhile,
  and seemed to get along
well enough, except . . .

Big Jim tended to
  boss Danny around—
get this, get
  that, pick up,
put down.

Danny was a
  good worker—
an experienced hand—
  he did not seem to resent
the unnecessary commands.

And as he said nothing
  the work went
well and was quickly
  done—Brazos View
had its potting shed.

The newspaper headline,
  a few weeks later—
Local Man Wins Lottery—
  must, for both men,
have come as quite a shock.

Danny had bought the
  winning ticket—and when
queried about his job and
  future plans, had announced
to the world, *I quit!*

Big Jim and Danny (with Brindle and me)

The Early Years

Before
   the larger house
was built
   we often took
our evening meals
   out at the pergola.
If there was
   an evening chill
we made a fire
   with cedar wood;
for light we had
   antique lamps,
for cooking
   a charcoal grill.

The air soft
   as night closed in,
crickets began their
   evening sounds
and fireflies (a few)
   floated around.
We stayed out until the
   Courthouse tower clock
struck too late
   an hour—
then packing up
   the aftermath
of our simple fête,
   went back in, to bed.

Jardin Potager

Mid March,
  the soil tilled,
seeds and plants
  planted according to
her plan—Dominique's
  kitchen garden
lies ready for
  the growing-season
ahead.

Carrots, peas,
  lettuce, chard,
broccoli and potatoes;
  radishes, onions,
turnips, tomatoes,
  borage and thyme—
the tumble of names
  declaring
it's springtime.

. . . awaiting alike
  that essential moment,
when energies
  intrinsic in sun
water and soil combine,
  releasing the life-
force encapsulated
  within—as
germination begins.

The emergent
  force—a bean sprout,
with a mud cap
  on its head one
hundred times the weight
  of its seed—
straining upward for
  sunlight and air in
Dominique's garden here.

Pergola and Potting Shed

The Garden Party

You are cordially
 invited to a
Garden Party . . .
  the first weekend
in June, the year after
  our lawn and gardens
were in.

Music and
 Garden buffet,
Six to eight p.m.
  The weather cleared
just in time,
  the evening air
was cool.

Champagne and
 light fare,
a flute and
  classical guitar . . .
fifty-five guests
  in all, came
to savor Brazos View.

The hostess, lovely in
 her wide-brimmed straw,
was pleased to hear
  what every hostess
hopes to hear—*delightful*—
  wonderful—most memorable
evening of the year.

Dominique and Pergola Roses

The New Garden Show
(Organic Roses)

Among rosarians
   there is a saying
about antique climbing roses;
   First year they sleep,
second year they creep,
   third year, they leap.
So it was at Brazos View:
   within a few years
Dortmunds climbed our fences,
   Rêve d'Or graced the pergola,
Climbing Pinkie, an almost
   continuous bloomer, spread
along our blufftop rails and
   hid some *awkward places.*

Beginning with first plantings
   in the courtyard of our
weekend house, roses became
   something of a passion
for Dominique. Catalogs,
   reference books and helpful
nursery folk moved the cause
   along. A consultant was
employed, who later became
   a friend. Although the
existing arrangement of this
   courtyard was a given,
the new planting scheme did
   much to enhance the space.

By spring of our fourth year
   gardens and flowers
had really taken hold, the
   pergola almost smothered
in blooms of peachy-gold,
   the yard barn transformed
by Climbing Pinkies and even
   some bluffside areas were
in bloom, with Cherokee Rose
   alongside the stone stair,
a swamp rose at a seep
   beneath the boulder there
and Mike's deep burgundy rose
   nodding out over the lake.

When our consultant friend
   later returned to review
the developing plan,
   she was impressed enough to
suggest featuring Brazos View
   on a weekly PBS television
program which she hosted, called
   The New Garden Show.
The program would focus on
   Dominique's organically grown
heritage roses, those vigorous
   nineteenth and early twentieth
century varieties, popular
   in old Southern gardens.

Sober Farm Couple

American Gothic

A small bunch (eight
  ounces in weight)
of Georgia Jet
  slips
made three rows,
  yielding
at harvest
  two hundred
pounds of sweet
  potatoes.

Pride
  got the better
of us and we
  had pictures
taken—*American
  Gothic*, we
said—really
  though, just
a case of
  harvest pride.

That was the
  best year;
weather and
  soil pests
took the next,
  and we
scaled back
  on our
country-style
  largesse.

Then, year
  after that
the nutrias came—
  a mother and
three kits—
  foraging
at night; a nip
  here, a bite
there, until so many
  potatoes were lost.

Brazos Berries

I have just come in
   from berry picking at
our garden berry patch,
   fingers stained purple-
red and a thorn embedded
   in my thumb—
the blackberries
   are at their prime.

Vines dry and ragged
   throughout much of the year
(a painful nuisance at times),
   come alive in spring
with green new growth
   and prim, white flowering—
prelude to the lustrous
   ebony, tart-tasty fruit.

How a Harvest Feels

If only from
   a garden plot
a harvest
   makes you proud,
the produce
   round, warm
and full, firm
   and ripe and
bright with colors
   from the sun.
The earth smell,
   moist, rich,
and clean.
   The tastes,
fresh, tart,
   real.

Though soil, seed,
   rain and sun
are due the credit,
   no harvest happens
without toil . . . .
   Is all of this what
makes harvesting
   feel so good
you want to
   write a poem,
or is it what
   we learn—
that harvest
   is the only way
of being sure
   we know the sun?

The Potting Shed

The potting shed—
   the magic of its musty
air, the moist redolence
   of composted earth and
the natural ground
   breathing up through
its graveled floor;
   sturdy seedlings in plastic
trays spread along
   the potting bench,
miracles of germination and
   of sun's light shared—
with Mike's logbook, pencils
   and coffee mug there.

Memorable Firsts

Our first garden harvest,
   squash, cucumbers,
tomatoes and peas,
   vines and plants
loaded with the promise
   of more . . .
never had vegetables
   tasted as sweet before.

That first year
   our irises rose up
so vigorous and tall,
   the rhizomes having been
blanketed with manure—
   flower plumes
elegant and refined,
   fragrance subtle, sublime.

The first spring
   the martins came
and brightened our lives—
   we had waited
as eagerly as children
   awaiting a holiday time—
the aerial shows they
   bring to our skies.

We called our first boat
   Beau Geste, a gift
the former owner left behind.
   It bounced and bobbed about
on the waves
   as we set out first time
to explore, going up to find
   where the river comes in.

Our first Fourth,
   seen from the deck
overlooking the lake;
   hundreds of people in
boats below, here to watch
   the town's fireworks show.
Incredible display,
   the *News* declared next day.

The first night
   we slept outside,
on the deck
   above the lake—
night sounds
   kept us awake;
owls, wind and water, and
   a bird calling to its mate.

Points of Light

Points of Light

A small cedar barn
    was built
some sixty feet
    from the house,
with one large window
    on its west side
and a smaller window
    on the east.

Built for storage
    of lawn equipment,
ladders, tools and such,
    rough wooden shelving
spans the larger window
    for display of the
collection of bottles
    found about the place.

Rich mahogany brown
    and green
(beer and soft drinks),
    blue and purpled
(tinctures and nostrums
    now extinct)—
sunlit, become jeweled
    points of light.

Sunrise

From the time
  the sun-fire
breaks over
  the low ridge
southeast of here,
  until the red-
orange orb that
  wakes the world
is seen entire,
  takes
slightly less than
  one hundred eighty
seconds of our
  lives.

Irises Brought In

Dominique has cut
  and brought irises
in, for fragrance
  and to shelter them
from wind—three glorious
  stems with multiple
blooms, rich butter-yellow
  and lavender blooms.
Fragile petals and
  furls, delicate and
graceful as the upturned
  hands of oriental
dancing girls.

Window Shopping

A female hummingbird
  hovers just beyond
the window glass,
  staring fixedly
at the flounced
  petals of the
wine and pink
  gladiolus inside . . .
avidly as a girl
  staring through
a shop window
  at an evening
dress.

Nell's Rose

We planted
   Nell's rose
against the low
   stone wall
built around the well
   hand-dug one
hundred years ago.

The mother plant in
   our neighbor's yard,
from which its
   cutting came,
was reliably known
   to be the equal of
that well in age.

This type of rose
   grows by suckering—
the plant itself, not
   so pretty—but
its numerous lavender-
   pink, tightly tufted
   flower rosettes are nice.

As notably delicate
   as any rose,
with a distinctive
   lemon-pepper scent—
we fondly named it
   in honor
of our neighbor-friend.

Window At Top Of The Stair

Window at top
  of the stair
squares the sky,
  concentrates
its hues;
  intensified blue,
as summer clouds
  astonishingly white
sail by,
  filling the stairwell
with a natural light.
  Southward facing,
noontime and night
  sun or moon
may penetrate our lives,
  with the brightness
of their light;
  as seasons pass
in slow parade . . .
  the window
at top of the stair.

An Upper Room

Roses the color
  of cream
in a crystal vase
  on a glass table,
overlooking the lake
  glittering back at
the sun . . . and at
  you and me.
Music . . . Vivaldi
  resonates in the room,
the air,
  crisp and clean
through open window sash,
  brings sounds of water
cascading down
  the boulders of the bluff;
a moment like a dream,
  just for you and me,
as we kiss.

Prism

A prism
  placed
in our high
  arched window
refracts the sun's
  early rays,
ornamenting
  walls and ceiling
of our upper room
  with patches
of prismatic light . . .
  all the colors
of the rainbow
  within that
colorless light.

Sitting Out

Shadow patterns,
    leaves
on shades
    drawn
against moonlight
    too bright
for sleep . . .
    after sitting
out so late.

Summer winds
    roll in
over the lake
    and up
the bluff's steep
    face, pleasantly
warm, fragrant,
    soft as velvet
to the skin.

Under the elm
    that roots beneath
our fossil stones
    is where
we sit, Dominique,
    Brindle, and I;
relaxed, mesmerized,
    washed in wind
and lunar light.

The moon's
    spare face,
luminous and clean,
    gleams
above the glittering
    sheen
it spreads across
    the lake
tonight.

Wind Chimes

Wind chimes hang
  from a hackberry limb
extending out over
  the bluff—
the sounds are
  soft and mellow,
low, velvety tones sifting
  into the bedroom above,
soft and gentle
  as the wind,
with a pattern
  random as the wind
drifting in and out
  of our consciousnesses
as we lie together
  this early Sunday morning,
half awake, half asleep.

Winter Shine

As the sun
    slides southward
in wintertime,
    its reflection
off the water
    of the lake
sparkles and
    dazzles and
shines—almost
    blindingly
at times.

Turning
    from the gallery-
hall into
    our main room
(with its tall
    glass walls),
any noontime
    when the sun's fully
intense and revealed
    quite takes one's
breath away.

Snow Light

Snow Light

... almost Valentine's,
    and it snowed
all day today,
    anything
beyond the lake
    obscure and gray.

Brazos View
    suffused
in snow light,
    white and
gray, with snow
    in piles today.

Our smaller trees
    bent low
as shrubs—yaupon,
    willow and cedar—
now all in powdery
    display.

Animal tracks
    clearly show,
and Brindle,
    running that funny
way she runs whirls
    and bounds away.

Nandina berries,
    in green
and ice surrounds,
    red and
bright as blood
    are found.

Inside out,
    each window
a wintery scene—
    icebound castle
from upper rooms to
    ice-clad lawns below.

A far corner (at dusk)
    viewed from our
dining room—
    becomes a lamplit
grotto, with softly
    dampened light at play.

Snow light
    outside,
firelight in—
    and snowing
still, at end
    of a beautiful day.

Brazos Walls

Old Brazos Walls

If walls could
   talk,
and paths
   and roads with
trees overshadowing,
   bridges that clatter
when driven over,
   or streams
driven through at
   low water crossings . . .
if walls could talk.

But walls do talk,
   and paths and
roads and old-time
   bridges, as
clearly as the water
   flowing ever on . . .
life has been,
   and will be,
yet never was
   or is, exactly
as it seems.

Brazos Church

The sun's
  just risen,
southeast
  across the lake;
beyond the
  buildings clustering
the bypass route,
  atop the ridge
of land that rises
  toward Comanche Peak,
stands a single
  structure,
with a steeple
  above its copper roof.

Even at
  this remove—
there's something special
  about that church;
not sect, not
  deity it
seems to me
  but the
hope
  and work
of so many
  hands
reaching, reaching
  toward the sky.

The Town Square

One block from
    Brazos View
is the town's historic
    Square . . . a quadrangle
with some dozen two-story
    business structures on
each side and a large
    stone, European style
county Courthouse (circa 1891)
    holding center stage.
Pictures extant
    show the Square's
unpaved central plane
    crowded with buggies,
wagons, horses and mules,
    and numerous
country folk
    in town for
market day, as well.

Many of the buildings
    look today much
as they did then, though
    the changes in
usage tell how the
    town has changed:
groceries, dry goods, hardware,
    saloons, blacksmith, livery
stables and buggy shops
    have given way to
antiques, cards and novelties,
    ice cream, restaurants and
a wine-tasting shop
    (mostly for tourist trade).
Besides the Courthouse,
    the bank's still here,
the Opera House and the old
    stone jail (a museum
today).

The Courthouse Clock

The ornamented
    gray, metallic
quadrilateral tower
    of the Courthouse
can be seen from
    our upstairs rooms—
each side with the face
    of a clock; one
clock, four faces.
    A sober
durable old device,
    in place from the time
the great stone structure
    first was built.

Wound weekly
    for all the years since;
steady and essential
    to the way the town lived,
it could be seen and heard
    almost anywhere within
the small community
    clustered around the Square.
Its sound muffled now
    (a renovation of the tower),
its soft, slow tones
    still count the hours,
reminding us of times past,
    assuring us of time to come.

The People Go Deep

Rooted it seems,
    deep as the deepest
rooted trees (liveoak, pecan,
    mesquite) . . . and
just as fixed
    in place.
The people here
    go deep,
back through the
    tough times,
long before the lake
    was in,
through two world
    wars and a Great
Depression in between.

Shortly after we
    bought this place
Glenn Etta, whose
    blue eyes and lively spirit
belied her ninety years,
    came to tell us
how Brazos View
    had once been.
We stood
    by the stone chimney
her grandfather built
    with mortar made from
river sand,
    now the centerpiece
of our pergola.

The great flu epidemic
    of 1918 had
taken Glenn Etta's
    mother, and her
grandparents took her
    in . . . a six-acre
farmstead, windmill and
    well near the house
and fields for crops
    in the bottomland;
the well, hand-dug
    and stone-lined,
sixty-two feet deep,
    with water sweet
and clear and cold.

Right or wrong,
    along with some
ragged sheds we
    had taken the
old house down,
    to *open the property
up* . . . Glenn Etta
    seemed not to
take it amiss;
    the hearth
remained, the heart
    of the house,
with a hundred years
    of memories en-
crusting its old stones.

Cetacean

Halfway up the steep stone stair
  hard against the bluff,
an immense boulder there,
  in size and form
something like a whale.
  Barnacled and gray,
its fossilized hide
  a compression of time,
from an age when such
  stone was animate . . .
and myriad creatures
  swam the seas,
to live and die
  in an endless stream.

A composite of nature now,
  with great forward nose
and protuberant eye,
  enduring into more modern times,
when a whole world
  will not know
what it will not know . . .
  yet, one touch or
brush against this ancient form,
  and we may learn
to feel, to see
  the real that's lain so long,
and all unknown,
  deeply anchored here.

Stechtel

Our nearest neighbor
  west (now deceased)
was an old man of
  German descent.
A self-sufficient widower,
  often gruff
and occasionally crude.
  He doted on his
tidy lakeside place
  with its garden plots
and sloping lawn.
  His house was filled
with antique clocks, a
  valuable collection;
the striking of any hour
  an acoustical event.

Sit down and tell me
  some lies;
tales and exploits were revived.
  The 300-pound grouper
fish (proof of which when
  I had scoffed produced
a picture), the countless
  deer he had killed,
the difficulties encountered
  trying to gain the approval
of Lucille's dad; then
  the drowning of his only son,
Just there off shore,
  on Thanksgiving Day,
as the family, disbelieving,
  looked helplessly on.

Now it's only Whitey,
  Blackie and me;
his two cats, his clocks,
  gardens and boathouse
dock down by the lake;
  where by choice, not
necessity, he took his baths
  twice each week—
a rumpled towel and
  bar of soap were
kept there. Seasonally
  his birds were also there,
the purple martins whose arrival
  each spring he awaited
with the eagerness of a child.
  We miss that old man.

Once he told me
  he had trained
his itinerant birds
  to dive through the hoop
of his upraised arms—
  who can say
if this was true.
  There was a workroom
in the house, where
  he meticulously worked
at repairing his clocks;
  but Stechtel's sanctuary
was his boathouse dock,
  boat ready and gear
arranged . . . a fisherman still,
  at his age.

A Further Word
About the Rock, Cetacean

Could this be
  the selfsame rock
against which the
  boy leaned to
catch his breath,
  near enough now
the top of the bluff
  to hear the murmured
talk of two jailers
  guarding the
rude little jail at night?

This was Cooney
  Mitchell's boy
his pony left tied
  some distance back
in the darkness
  of the river bend,
his small, taut
  body pressed hard
against the great rock,
  . . . no way they's
goin' to hang my pap.

Had he made a plan,
  or just grabbed a
weapon at the bunkhouse
  door, jumped astride
his pony and raced
  up the long road
from the Mitchell family
  compound, at a loop-back
of the river some eight
  miles to the south
of the new county seat?

Sixty feet up
  from the river's bed,
the rock was (and is) at
  a break in the bluff.
He hitched up
  his pants, shinned
over the top and . . .
  the jailer probably
fired blind, a shot that
  tore the night apart,
and left young Mitchell dead.

The hanging of Cooney Mitchell, in 1874, was "the only hanging under legal proceedings" to take place in Hood County, Texas.

The result of a land dispute between two local families that left two dead and one wounded, the actual hanging occurred elsewhere but the little jail in which Mitchell had awaited hanging was located near the brow of the bluff, here at Brazos View.

Brazos Pathing

Good sense travels on well-worn paths; genius never.
— C. Lombroso (1836-1909)
. . . ask for the old paths, where is the good way, and walk therein.
— Jeremiah, VI: 16

It seems perfectly reasonable
　　that differences of opinion prevail
concerning the paths
　　in the side yard here . . .
habit or convenience or necessity.

The shortest line
　　between two points
is not a curve
　　nicely rounding
the pomegranate tree.

Who first decides
　　where a path should go?
Grass cannot grow
　　when trodden so and
grass was meant to cover here.

Passing to one side
　　yields no improvement . . .
just presses down
　　more tender blades,
creating yet another path.

If we think so well
　　of the ways we walk
let's formalize the trails,
　　with stones or edging,
showing they were intended.

This then is how matters stand:
　　none of us seeming
to know for sure,
　　what to do concerning
the dilemma of our pathing.

The Peak

Comanche Peak,
  the long, low
backdrop to our view
  out over the lake—
more mesa than peak,
  rising some hundreds
of feet above the rolling
  countryside, its
rocky, wooded flanks
  topped with several
hundred acres of flat
  open grazing land.

It is said
  the Comanches
called this rocky butte
  Que tah to yah, and
considered it a sacred
  refuge place,
where women and children
  could safely stay as
the tribe's warrior braves
  rode out
to hunt and raid,
  as far away as Mexico.

The Peak is
  owned privately now
(fenced, gated, locked);
  late spring each year
the public is invited in,
  for a picnic and bonfire
benefiting a community cause.
  *Seven counties can be
seen*, the Square, and the
  lake's loops and bends;
south, alongside Squaw Creek,
  the nuclear plant looms.

Mid-century, Texian
  independence won
and statehood gained a
  powwow of local tribes and
government representatives
  was convened,
atop Comanche Peak—
  with speeches, food and
gifts exchanged, a several
  days' encampment ensued
which seemed to hold
  some promise of peace.

But tide of events
  ran too strong—
population pressures,
  divergent cultures,
and human nature
  unpeaceable at its
core—Comanche,
  Apache, Lipan,
Waco, Kiowa, Caddo,
  Tonkawa, Wichita; the
ancient Plains Indian peoples
  too soon were no more.

Visitors to the Peak
  want to see
Signature Rock—
  names, dates, initials
carefully carved in stone,
  the early settlers here,
finding their refuge
  on Comanche Peak;
less than a generation after,
  as a young brave alone,
Quanah Parker had come,
  seeking his *spirit guide*.

A Bit About What Lies Below

Beneath the surface soil
   we garden in,
beneath the yard where
   Brindle plays,
beneath the rock and clay
   Brazos View is built upon,
the deeper world begins;
   alternating layers,
limestone, sandstone, shale,
   sediment of antique seas
laid down so long ago,
   repository now
of sand, gravel,
   water, coal and oil.
Earth's crust, it's called,
   at some thousands of
feet deep is yet near
   nothing compared to the
caldron world still
   farther below;
upper mantle
   to inner core,
several thousand miles of
   increasingly compressed,
increasingly hot magmatic
   rock, with solid magnetic
iron at the core . . .
   our far-flung
spinning globe, wrapped
   around an enormous
fiery-hot ball of iron.

A Part Wild Place

Wildness

A wildness of wind
   and water is
in our lives today,
    with wind in wintry
gusts roiling the bay,
    the water leaden
the sky gray,
    and workboats tied
against the lee;
    gulls cry and slide
sideways to the wind,
    geese, a skein,
with haunting calls
    penetrate the air,
southward on their way;
    whitecaps top the waves,
the water's turned
    to spume . . .
there's a wildness
    in our lives today.

A Scavenging Pair

While I nodded, nearly napping,
Suddenly there came a tapping,
As of someone rapping
At my chamber door.
"'Tis some visitor, " I muttered,
"Tapping at my chamber door:
Only this and nothing more."
—Poe

Yet it was
  more, much
more . . . not
  rapping or
tapping but bumping
  and thumping
heavily, against
  my library door.

Two great
  black birds
(buzzards), the larger
  lunging
with persistent brute
  force against
the glass of the
  sliding door.

Its more clever
  mate pressed so
hard at the low
  east window screen,
it spread her breast
  feathers out . . .
what bizarre behavior
  was this?

Standing now
  just inside,
I shooed them off;
  but had
no sooner turned
  my back than
they came on again,
  resuming their attack.

Close to,
  wings outspread,
a black buzzard's
  huge . . . when
I dropped the shades,
  they backed off
and after a while
  flapped away.

With wooden slatted
  arms as ribs,
and rough, rawhide
  leather seat, my
favorite reading chair
  (four feet inside the
glass) must to them have
  looked like carrion.

Bird Watching
At Brazos View

Considering the complexity
   of our human psyches,
one is well-advised
   not to anthropomorphize
animal behavior. Yet, among
   the birds at Brazos View
we see courting, bonding,
   mating, nest building,
care and feeding of the young,
   fledging, empty nesting,
health, harmony and good seasons
   filled with song; also
territoriality, nest robbing,
   multiple mates, fighting,
inattentive parenting, sickness
   death and harder times
when the seasons turn—
   activities all similar to
activities the news of which we
   focus on in our daily papers.
Psyches notwithstanding, there is
   so much of us alive in nature
and so much of nature alive in us
   that a lot we need to know
can be learned watching birds.

Fishing

Blue-black
  against the leaden
waters of late
  afternoon
our great heron
  stands offshore
like a statue
  on the stub
of a half-sunken tree
  waiting for schooling
shad to pass by.

Motionless, waiting
  patiently—
then the thrust,
  quick,
and the shad
  wriggling
in that rapier-beak
  glints
in the late
  afternoon light—
and disappears.

Breakfasting

The big ash
   nearest the house,
alive with
   birds today,
birds breakfasting
   on the tiny worms
that devour
   spring leaves
of the tree.

A young pair
   of blackcapped
chickadees
   busily search out
and feed on
   the worms,
one never
   losing sight
of the other.

Barely two ounces
   weight each,
to windstorm, predators
   or accident
they are prey, yet
   will nest and lay
and fledge, and live
   to forage
another spring.

Gulls

Gulls fly in
   to glean the shad
dying or dead
   from the lake's
recent algae bloom.

They turn, cry
   and dive,
cleaving the air
   like arrowheads
against the sky.

Life for life
   in the abstract
may seem okay, but
   is not so pretty
in light of day.

And begs the questions
   —how, and why—
this myriad of
   life was
made to die?

A Secret Garden

At the brow
   of the bluff,
beneath our
   terrace wall,
a bramble patch
   of brier and
wild forsythia,
   where the
smallest birds
   come to rustle
among fallen leaves
   and low, winter grass.

Out of the wind
   in lee of the house,
safe from a neighbor's
   prowling cats and the
gray hawk that patrols
   the wooded slopes
along our shore—
   red birds, wrens,
sparrows, chickadees—
   a bramble patch,
a secret garden
   for the birds.

Raid On the Hackberry Tree

From that same
   bramble patch—
sanctuary of the
   smaller birds—
our resident mockingbird
   sallies forth in defense
of his stash
   of winter berries.

The hackberry nearby
   is his, the
swamp holly at foot
   of the stair as well
(the pyracantha, too).
   Humans, dogs, even
squirrels can come and
   go as they please.

Yet, let more
   than one or two
berry-eating birds
   come through
and, *Mr. Mocker's*
   in a stew . . .
which was the case
   just yesterday.

Unrivaled in trimness
   of appearance, the
dapper cedar waxwing
   also has,
for berries,
   an insatiable appetite
. . . not good news
   for mockingbirds.

Wintering waxwings
   fly in flocks,
thirty, forty, fifty
   ravenous birds.
In a few minutes' time
   trees full of berries
can be stripped
   nearly clean.

The hackberry,
   suddenly alive with
birds, our mocker
   dives right in;
a bunch here, a
   bunch there—he rushes,
they retreat, but leave
   the branches bare.

Shadow Birds

To live
　where the shadow
of the buzzard passes
　slow and even
over the land,

to hear
　the hiss
of wind
　through
outspread wings,

to see
　an underwing
go gray
　banking back
away from the sun,

to know
　the sky
sustains
　and earth
provides,

to recognize,
　the singular
importance of
　these silent
shadow birds.

Cormorant

Black wings
   against a gray
sky,
   solitary,
purposeful,
   beating steadily
northward,
   to live,
to breed
   . . . to fly:
and never
   the question,
why?
   Black wings
against a gray
   sky,
steadily beating
   northward.

After the Storm

Through broken
   clouds
a waning moon
   spills an undulating
lacquered sheen
   on the surface
of the lake, the air
   still and clean
after the storm . . . which
   began late afternoon,
a terrific thunderclap,
   with wind
instantly upon us,
   and rain,
thrashing the spring leaves
   of the trees.
Then, the hail began;
   a few pecks at first
against the window glass,
   increasingly loud
until everything seemed
   a madness of racket
and wind . . . surely
   the great elm
overarching the lake
   would go down,
surely flowers
   and garden plantings
would be beaten
   to the ground.
Where could our birds
   find refuge
in such a storm?
   As quickly almost
as it had come,
   it was gone;
and the moon rose
   to pour its
watery light
   over the scene.

Night Alarm

Brindle sounded
  the alarm,
her deep voice
  reverberating
off the high
  bluff's walls,
her hackles
  half raised up,
her head pointed
  in direction of . . .
first one dark
  shape, then
another (silhouetted
  in the moonlight),
scurrying up the
  slanting trunk of
a hackberry tree.
  Sensing this to be some-
thing not too threatening,
  Brindle soon slacked off
and returned to where

we three had been sitting,
  savoring the moon
and an evening breeze.
  Then, another ominous
bark and
  just beyond in
our tallest chinaberry . . .
  not two but several
dark smudges against
  the lighter sky;
three, four, five, and
  one (larger) six,
raccoons up a single tree.
  Their bandit faces
facing all in our
  direction, showed less
alarm than impatience
  (for us to be gone) . . .
leaving them alone
  there, high in that
tall berry tree.

The Indifference of Turtles

One must admire
  the indifference
of the turtle,
  emerging just now
from the murk
  of its two-months'
sleep . . .embedded
  in mud
at bottom
  of the lake,
neither food nor
  light nor air
as winter storms
  raged and
temperatures dropped,
  the turtle
slept.

Why should it
  not regard me
indifferently . . .
  ten thousand times
longer than man
  its clan has
survived, more
  secure by far
in its carapacial
  niche?
Before birds,
  before the seas
which laid our boulders
  down, and long before
mammals in anything like
  modern form,
turtles were around.

Opheodrys Aestivus

As elegant
  as a woman's
necklace,
  a green snake
lies languidly
  among the juniper
boughs—

as green as
  spring leaves
against the darker
  green; three
seasons now
we have
  seen it here.

Opheodrys aestivus,
  elegance and
indolence—
  or so it seems,
this lovely, slender
  serpent, foraging
among the shrubs.

Sunning

A turtle sunning
  at one end
of the boulder
  Brindle launches from
plops unceremoniously
  into the water
ahead of her,
  then comes up
to look around.

Its primordial head,
  seeing me,
seeing her,
  drops down again,
then reappears—
  do we seem so
strange a pair,
  or does it merely
want the sun again?

A Part Wild Place

Racoon, nutria, fox,
  possum, squirrel,
snake, turtle, armadillo,
  beaver and mole;
heron, gull,
  osprey, owl,
turkey, wood duck,
  hawk and crow—
long periods of
  habitation by
the human race
  notwithstanding,
Brazos View
  remains today
a part wild place.

At Night

Things happen
  at night
around here—
  feral cats and
our great-horned owl
  wait on
the slightest movement
  of moles underground.

Possums
  in their slow
primordial ways
  dig for grubs
along the lakeside path
  (uprooting
Dominique's spring bulbs
  we'll find next day).

Spider spin
  silken snares
before the moon
  and await
their prey—
  hunters and hunted
leave alike their lairs,
  all must forage to survive.

Bats, we rarely see
  but know
they are there,
  cats, or raccoons,
strip fish carcasses
  clean, down to
the bare skeletons later
  found along shore.

Out with Brindle
  for a late walk
a bird is startled
  from its rest—
how little we know
  of how, or where,
so many, many
  sleep.

The nocturnal world's
  a mysterious
world—mostly we
  are unaware
of what is astir
  outside, at night,
while inside
  we sleep.

Wind Patterns

Wind Patterns

1

Wind patterns
  on the water,
a kind of braille,
  not to touch
but for the mind
  to feel.

Ruffled lace
  and filigree,
puffs of
  wind
eddying beneath
  the bluff.

2

As waves heavy
  against
the opposite shore
  show
the full force
  of wind . . .

driving the water
  forward,
tumbling it into
  the cattails
and overtopping
  the windward walls.

Storm Front

Birds hurtle
  like bullets
through the air,
  trees heavy
with leaves bend
  to the ground,
clouds swollen
  rumble like great
embattled beings,
  lightning
cracks and flashes
  close by . . .
a storm front
  passes Brazos View,
the hiss of rain
  trailing behind.

The Aftermath

Wind and rain,
  a serious storm
yesterday,
  upriver from
Brazos View—
  the lake an unsightly
mess this morning,
  water the color
of café au lait,
  logs, limbs, trash
and other debris
  floating atop a
swollen current,
  a flood; and
the air heavy
  with an unpleasant
odor of decay.

We had planned
  to go out
in the boat today—
  Dominique, Brindle
and I—but not in
  water like this.
Yet it is spring,
  and a sunny
Sunday morning
  for some cannot
be denied; boats are
  out, tentatively
nosing through the flotage.
  One pulls alongside a
half-sunk tree trunk twenty
  feet long, then slowly
carefully, moves on.

Driftwood Pieces

Fifteen miles
  upriver from here,
the Brazos
  widens to several
miles of shoal water
  that boats barely
can pass through . . . the
  deeper river beyond
(approaching the lake)
  over many, many
years has brought
  the logs and limbs
of thousands of trees,
  to be left stranded,
an almost impenetrable jumble,
  stark, skeletal,
half in, half out of
  the water.

The river floods
  from time to time
loosening and lifting
  the logs (and
other debris), floating them
  down to lodge
lakeside here after
  the storm . . .
hacked, sawn,
  twisted and torn,
water-carved with curves
  and contours
to make any
  sculptor proud . . .
even covered
  with mud and slime,
something about them
  appeals.

Almost waterlogged,
  sizes ranging

large to small,
   all are difficult
to roll or drag ashore,
   to be left
in the sun
   to dry . . .
then, cleaned and
   dried again
the work begins;
   scraping, sanding,
every knot, crevice and
   curve, until the grain's
brought out again, and
   varnished to a satin sheen:
the driftwood sculptural pieces
   seen at Brazos View.

Driftwood Sculptural Piece

Sea Seine

This has been
   a sea of a day
with wind coming
   in waves
over our summer
   trees—a
day that drove and
   plunged in mounting
waves of wind . . .
   the kind of day
one cannot seine
   in any net of words
(nor even memory).

Petals

Blood-red petals
   of poppies
blown loose
   by the wind
sail erratically
   as butterflies,
and settle
   in the thicket
of plants
   sprung up
from our garden
   ground.

Thermals

Turning, circling,
   spiraling
silhouettes of birds
   rise, riding
an upward column
   of summer-warm
air visible
   only by the
rising column of birds.

At such height
   a four-foot span—
half the length
   of a fountain pen—
no movement of wing,
   soaring, soaring
to the base of
   massifs of cloud,
and then beyond.

Distant Storm

Clouds high
  and white
as the day
  drew in,
The air
  smelled
of rain—
  the moon,
near full,
  rising
as daylight
  grew dim.

Cumulous masses
  of clouds,
front-lit
  by the moon,
lightning pulsating
  from within, spanning
our southern sky—
  crickets stirred,
waves lapped gently
  at the shore,
a train's lonely call
  came drifting in.

The news,
  next day,
told the story—
  torrential rain
and hail,
  with *destructive*
wind; the capricious
  nature of such things—
not fifteen miles
  from Brazos View,
for us, just
  one dramatic scene.

Marking the Seasons

The tendency to
   regard with awe
an ability of
   the ancients
to accurately interpret
   positions of
the sun
   at given times
of the year,
   may somewhat
be misplaced . . .
   though one can
not overstate
   the importance of
familiarity with
   one's native space.

The sun's first
   rise at
autumnal equinox,
   centers precisely
in the narrow east
   window of our
bedroom window box.
   And at
summer solstice,
   the afternoon sun
first comes into
   the small north room
(upstairs), laying a band
   of light across its wall . . .
the seasons are marked so
   at Brazos View.

The Wind Relentless

The wind
  intense,
now three days,
  limbs
and leaves
  torn away.

The sound
  outside
buffets the ears,
  inside
sounds like
  the sea.

Wind chimes
  clang crazily,
yard cans and chairs
  blown about,
plants and grass
  wither and dry.

Our great heron
  sweeping by
barely manages
  to keep on course—
the wind relentless,
  three days now.

Eupatorium
A Butterfly Bush

At base of one
   of the boulders
bordering the lakeside path,
   a flowering shrub
with an odd name
   . . . eupatorium.
Dying back to its stalks
   at first hard freeze,
late to leaf out in spring,
   it will not flower
until fall.

When nights
   are crisp and long,
and the days late to warm,
   with asters, ruellias
and morning glories gone,
   to its clustered
purple flowers the butterflies come:
   Buckeyes, Viceroys, Monarchs
and Queens . . . a fluttering
   of feeding,
at the eupatorium.

Walking Sticks

First crisp day
  of fall
Daniel comes
  to trim and
thin our trees.
  Five seasons of
hot and dry
  have stressed them
seriously

Bores in the hackberries,
  dieback on the
limbs and leaf burn
  on the leaves
of the broad-leaved trees.
  Seventeen in all
will come down,
  yielding harvest
(of a kind).

Firewood, yes,
  in two-foot lengths,
elm, oak, cedar or pecan
  (with hackberry a
second, second best).
  For walking sticks,
any wood will do . . .
  the handle crook
is what one needs to find.

Of course, grain
  and straightness
and caliper are
  desired,
but a natural
  crook that marries
the hand is
  what you hope
to find.

With each limb
  that Daniel cuts,
I watch and
  wait—then
rush in, grab
  hold and
pull away quick—
  a sturdy
walking stick?

The first stick
  I ever made
I made when I
  was ten;
mesquite, with
  a gnarled top—
de-barked, dried,
  sanded and sealed—
for my dad.

First Winter Day

Gray
  gray
sky today,
  the air
bitter cold.
  Grass, frozen,
crackles and
  crunches
underfoot,
  icicles like
holiday ornaments
  hang from
the eaves,
  birds are at
the berry trees .
  . . first
winter day
  this year.

Mistletoe

One of the few
  natural things
disliked here at
  Brazos View
is mistletoe—
  particularly as it
afflicts our cedar elm
  and hackberry trees.

Of course we
  are happy
to have mistletoe
  at Christmastime,
its rich, green
  leaves and clustered
pearlescent berries, help
  the holiday glow.

But these same
  berries are poisonous
to dogs and children;
  and over time—
interrupting the sap's
  seasonal flow—
mistletoe will damage
  our deciduous trees.

A parasite,
  spread tree to
tree by the seed
  left in droppings
after the birds have fed—
  slowly it spreads,
almost as slowly as its
  host tree grows.

But full-blown, our
  winter trees
become mistletoe trees,
  deprived of
winter's rest—weakened
  and somewhat arthritic in
appearance, with knobby
  limbs and swollen joints.

Mistletoe removal
  is one of Mike's
winter jobs: up in the
  trees with a hook-ended
pole snapping off the
  parasitic stems, until
the ground is littered
  with mistletoe debris.

The Lake at Night

The lake
  at night,
in winter
  an inky slate,
the only markings
  the bypass lights,
red, green and gold;
  concentric pools
of reflected light,
  as fish feed
noisily in schools
  (brief respite
from winter's cold):
  the water
heaving gently
  shoreward,
then pushing back
  into night.

Cedar Smoke

Late

Have you seen
  any martins,
a neighbor wants to know;
  Not yet,
not yet, we say,
  the martins are
way late this year.

Valentine's Day
  has come and gone,
nest houses have
  been up a month
or more, the last
  freeze
occurred weeks ago.

We watch and
  listen each day—
they come in so high,
  often they will be heard
before they are seen—
  listening for
their bright cheery cries.

Imagine the distances
  they must travel—
each way, each year—
  just to do their
nesting here, imagine
  our loss, should
they not reappear.

On the Lake

*— the hiss of spray beside the boat, the
smell of cedar and of cedar smoke —*

Sun's fire spread
  across the sky,
or soft and vaporous
  in subtlest
shades and hues—
  sunsets
illuminate the clouds
  and draw us out
to view. . . .

Brindle comes
  too—her
excitement unbounded,
  yet she settles down
after awhile
  in the bow
with Dominique—
  barking now and again at
other boat dogs passing by.

Adventuring;
  up and back
overall forty miles,
  to where the river comes
in—past the stumps
  and mud flats and storm-
tossed trees,
  the boat slowed
and wallowing.

Or, bird watching,
  when the day's
heat breaks;
  buzzards' roost
up-lake, heron roost
  down, osprey sightings
and kingfishers in between;
  the rush of swallows as
we pass beneath the bridge.

. . . awaiting moonrise
  keeps us late, yet
what can equal
  slipping slowly
into that silver swath
  of scattered light
a low moon
  pours out
onto the lake.

Coming in
  past dark,
Brazos View seems
  grand anchored alongside
the shore—lit up like
  an ocean liner—
and as we align boat
  with boathouse,
Brindle signals us in.

Cedar Smoke

Many years now,
  in fact since
we first came
  to Brazos View,
evenings when we sit out
  or are on the lake
in our boat,
  we smell a sweet
fragrance of cedar smoke.

A gypsy fire,
  or kids camping out,
or some votive offering
  to the evening hour,
floating in from
  how many miles
away and from
  how much time
gone by?

Cedarwood smoke
  from an evening fire;
who can it be
  in this day,
what glint of eye
  or odd intent
sends
  such an incense
sailing our way?

Strangely Quiet

As summer solstice
    nears, still
no signs of martins
    this year.

The skies
    above Brazos View
seem strangely quiet
    now.

Geese with their
    high wild cries,
dove with their
    gentle tones—

jays' complaints
    and the wren's
sweet song, but no
    martins' cheery calls.

Chaste Tree

During the Middle Ages, monks were said to use
the foliage of this fragrant shrub
to enhance their meager beds.

Celibate souls of
　　those sad monks
must have suffered
　　twice over,
sleeping on its
　　sensual boughs—
sensual to the touch,
　　wickedly so,
and as well
　　to sense of smell.

In full bloom
　　now with
royal spikes
　　it roots just
opposite Cetacean's lair,
　　rising above
the great stone stair;
　　chaste tree,
vitex or
　　monk's pepper tree.

By some strange
　　inversion
anciently associated
　　with chastity,
more shrub than tree
　　its touch, sight and
fragrance do beguile,
　　and leave one
wondering how names
　　can deceive.

Desert Willow

Bumble bees
   black and yellow
tumble in and out
   of the flowers
on our desert willow.
   Small orchid-like
flowers with the
   subtlest scent
attracting not only
   the bees
but hummingbirds and
   butterflies as well.

The hottest days,
   the driest days
of midsummer
   our willow
is in bloom,
   reminding me of
lines from Thomas Gray's
   old poem lamenting,
Sweetness wasted
   on the desert air—
and I am glad to say, this
   is not true at Brazos View.

Brazos Waterfall

Rain running off
   the roof
became blocked behind
   the house—
we needed some way
   to let it drain
down to the lake.

The auto court
   had been put in
tilting east and
   east of the house
the soil was thin,
   underlain with
layers of rock.

The land drained
   naturally here
toward the bluff,
   water cascading
(when it rained enough)
   in a regular
little waterfall.

Two small ponds
   were planned
beneath the trees
   at our entry gate,
higher than the
   drainage channel;
the design was complete.

Water pumped
   from the lake
would fill the ponds
   to overflowing,
then via the rock-bottomed
   channel, over the bluff
and down to the lake.

Rocks: we had the
   natural rock for the
bottom of the flume,
   and boulders at the bluff,
edging, shouldering and
   finishing stones would
have to be brought in.

Mike and I went
   to the masons' yards,
scavenging for the rocks
   we might use—
and set to work
   in summer heat,
putting each stone in place.

Now, birds and squirrels
   (and Brindle)
come to drink and play,
   the water gurgles,
splashes and flows
   towards the bluff—
our Brazos waterfall.

Grass Fires

A dusky orange
   suffuses this morning's
early light
   as it did
last evening's
   sunset light.

High winds yesterday
   fanned grass fires
in the county
   north of here,
sending dust and smoke
   down our way.

The air gritty
   and acrid,
a pall overspreading
   so quickly
we barely got the house
   closed up in time.

The Cruelest Month

Eliot declared
    April the cruelest
month, *breeding lilacs*
    out of the dead land . . . .
August is that
    month at Brazos
View, when the rush
    of spring is
past and summer's
    ease has fled,
when fireflies
    and butterflies
have yielded center
    stage to the cicadas'
incessant chirr.
    This is our
cruelest month;
    birds droop,
flowers fade, leaves
    curl and fall
to the ground, the
    grass goes brittle
and brown . . .
    not a *wasteland*
to be sure,
    but a definite
lassitude does settle
    in, in August,
here at Brazos View.

Is There?

Is there a
   heart so
citified that
   the wild cry
of geese in flight
   or the fall
smell of wood-fire
   smoke can
not penetrate?

The Opposite Shore

A Winter Morning
(Layers of Perception)

Bitter cold
   this morning,
warmth lake waters
    stored all summer long
escapes in rising swirls
    into the air,
a diaphanous veil;
    our accustomed opposite
shore as strange and lovely
    as an oriental scene.
The sun burns through,
    a pallid yellow,
turning haze into
    a muted, yellow glow.

A high fork
    of our great elm
(well above the mist),
    in full sun
a squirrel, brown and warm,
    nibbles at a nut
earlier secreted there;
    higher still, a
single, white vapor trail
    against the spatial blue,
a sparkling silver bullet
    penetrates the air . . .
layers of perception,
    in a winter morning's cold.

The Stray

Water rising
   after the heavy
rains must have
   loosed it
to ride
   high and level
nearshore here
   on the lake.

Looking lost
   and lonely
as any stray—
   someone's canoe
set adrift,
   current, waves and
wind at cross-purposes
   about its fate.

Up the bluff's
   steep steps
headed for the cedar
   barn, Brindle and I
ran ... a rope, a rake
   and a wooden block
ought to
   do the trick.

We slid and
   scrambled
down the bank
   to water's edge—
Brindle in water
   up to her chest
and I near
   knee deep.

The rope
   knotted around
the wooden block
   made a lariat
of sorts, and heaved
   way out fell
into the boat,
   and held.

We had our prize—
   a gentle tug,
it turned as easily
   as an animal
on a lead and
   came our way—
the rake we used
   to beach....

A London Morning

On days like
    today
one might be
    anywhere
the world
    gone blank
and gray,
    our opposite
shore erased away.

The fog crept
    slowly in,
until the view
    from upstairs
became a chalkboard
    wiped clean,
and nothing,
    nothing but gray
could be seen.

Except the mind
    has its ways—
and out of the mist
    images rise,
of memories there—
    Picadilly, Soho
and Hyde Park, with
    the Queen's own Guard
on parade today.

A Fossil Found

A small fragment
   of fossil,
its shallow contour
   held fast
within a matrix—
   of dullish color,
a pebble at our feet.

A pebble
   of awkward shape—
nondescript,
   of no intent.
Yet, bringing forward
   our most
ancient times.

Its concavity
   so clearly showing
flutings of the shell,
   tell which
family was this
   coming down to us
today. . . .

The reverse of
   nature,
not giving way,
   showing its image
upon the ground—
   for passersby
a fossil found.

Hammerstone

. . . river and prairie stretch ahead,
a good, hard stone is found,
it takes a tool to make a tool,
this he long had known.

Some things
  must be taken
a priori—
  my hand fits
as his would have,
  a human warmth
is in the stone.
  Thumb, fore and
middle fingers cradle it
  in the palm—
a rock tool,
  ready to hone.

A hand the size
  of mine he
would have had,
  for tasks he knew
which I know not,
  flaking and dressing
his points of flint.
  Skill in the hand,
work in the stone—
  which tribe was his
as he sat cross-legged here,
  he would not work alone.

Angularities
(At Dawn)

Cloud bank
　low and gray
angles down across
　our eastern sky
at break of day —
　makes the lake
a darkened plane;

a buoy light
　marking the mid-channel
line perfectly aligns
　the morning star
and a light ashore—
　a triangular figure
against the sky;

its landward angle
　paralleling the slant
of cloud and
　the wake of
a solitary waterbird—
　a chevron of
geese passes overhead;

making the world
　seem to be
angling all one way,
　but another cloud
another day—
　or other birds may
turn it right around.

The 4th

The Nation yes,
   in its ideals
and aspirations,
   freedom and
equality . . . yes.
   On parade, red
white and blue,
   banners and bunting
salute the Nation, yes.
   Children on decorated
wagons and bikes,
   as sirens wail and
the music plays on,
   volunteer firemen
and a high school band.
   Floats pass by,
a church, a charity, a
   patriotic theme; P.T.A.,
4-H and F.F.A. to
   the rattle of applause.
A veteran straightens,
   as colors of the Guard
unfurl in a breeze
   at a corner of the Square.
The vintage courthouse
   centered there, affirms
a Nation, yes.

Looking Out

A window of
   a second floor
room here
   looks down
onto the end
   of Brazos Street.
Our neighbor Nell's
   tidy place
is to the right,
   the old church
property to the left.

Brazos Street
   intersects Pearl,
a short half-block away,
   the town's mayor's
handsome *old vickie*
   on one corner and
the Langdon Cultural Center
   across the way.
A network of limbs—
   pecan and ash—
screens our view.

But we can
   gauge the traffic
on Pearl and
   see the approach
of the mail carrier each day,
   watch for deliveries
or guests
   at the gate,
know when the trash men
   come—our window
on the world.

Amaranthus

Our amaranths
   finally have
raised their burgundy
   heads above the
garden rails,
   princes' plumes;
surviving summer's heat
   they stand now
eight feet tall,
   nodding luxuriantly in
the lighter air of fall.

Several millennia
   before our kind
came to this western sphere,
   our forerunners here
knew the age-old
   secrets of *Amaranthus*—
leaf and seed.
   Huauhtli, it was called,
symbol of immortality,
   sacred to the rites
of the Aztecs' priests.

Thunder Over Texas

Ten Thousand Bikers Coming to Town

Raw, ragged
  rumbling,
Thunder Over Texas
  rolls down Pearl Street
to the Square,
  the Christian Bikers
are in town.

Bikes sparkling
  and clean,
chrome and metallic
  sheens line
the cordoned Square,
  Levi's and leather,
blue and black everywhere.

Testimonials on the
  sidewalk, Kool Aid
in the shade, tattooed
  crosses and deep-
tanned faces and arms,
  black head-scarves
like pirates wore.

The police are
  out in force,
religious rally
  notwithstanding,
but the women are stout,
  the men tamed, with
many a grizzled mane.

Rain late afternoon
  cleared before
evening services
  at City Park began—
the amplified music
  and voices drifting
down to us here.

. . . waiting for
  the motors' mighty
roars to rip the air
  after, each engine
a thunderclap, exploding
  power, as the host
of bikers rev up to go.

Understorying

… the husbandman waiteth … and hath long patience for it …
—James 5:7

Wind racing
    across the lake
and up the bluff
    funnels between
the buildings here.

Three mature ash and
    a half-grown cedar elm
hold the rocky space
    between our large house
and the smaller one.

Especially when leaves
    are full the wind
bends, whips and
    often snaps the brittle
ash tree limbs.

Limbs overhanging the houses
    have become a concern, and
when Daniel comes this year
    we may have to remove the
largest of these trees.

Our first days here,
    one-tenth the size
it is today I saw a small
    tree—and decided then
to let it live in the understory.

. . . the understory of this
    same larger tree; beginning
a practice followed since
    of *understorying* our
problematic trees.

Volunteer, or transplant, the
    canopy overhead will hold
it back, but slow and steady
    the young grow on, ready
when the time has come.

Gradually (over many years)
    short-lived or disease prone
trees will be replaced
    by stronger, longer lasting,
more attractive ones.

Understory offers sanctuary, too,
    for sun-shy smaller trees
and shrubs—dogwood, redbud,
    Japanese maple, yaupon—
quince, hydrangea and berry shrubs.

Partial, filtered and seasonal
    light must be taken
into account—everything needs
    some sun; the basic
rule for understorying.

Importance of a River

Place-names significant
  in early Texas history
are associated with the Brazos.
  San Felipe de Austin, Texas'
first Anglo-American colony,
  Brazoria and Velasco,
its first ports of entry,
  and Washington-on-the-Brazos,
where independence from Mexico
  would be declared.
The river, navigable then,
  with its rich alluvial plain,
moderate weather and ample rain
  proved the empresario's
(Austin's) representations right.

More than a century before
  the Texians came, Spanish
explorers had named the river
  Brazos de Dios—and
centuries before the Spaniards,
  for native, tribal groups
living or camping
  along the stream,
the river was life's blood.
  Its uninterrupted flow
meant life could be sustained—
  not by water alone but with
fish, fowl and game as well;
  the river (like sun and rain
and air), essential for them.

The Brazos—
  much changed today:
several large lakes (important
  reservoirs) hold back its flow,
providing flood control, electric
  power, water supply,
sports, recreation, and home-
  building sites; adversely
affecting its natural condition,
  the water often clouded with
the effluvia of denser habitation
  and silt from erosion or the
digging of rock and sand—
  only at the dams do waters
run anything like pristine.

The river at Brazos View,
  swallowed by the lake;
yet its current can be seen
  after heavy rains or when
water's released at the gates.
  Knowing the current remains,
focuses and connects so many
  things: the tilt of the land
is seen, the importance
  of the elements shown, and
our connection to times past
  and times forward is known—
this river, together with our
  skies, birds and rocky bluffs,
is why we are, at Brazos View.

The Law

Brindle and I
　were at the
compost pile,
　cranking the handle
of the finishing drum—
　when suddenly
she became alert
　and bolted
round the corner
　of our new workshop
building there,
　barking, barking,
her loudest alarm.

. . . following after,
　to see what
the fuss was about,
　I was quite
surprised to see
　two police officers pre-
paring to scale our fence.
　One male, one
female, in their
　yellow safety jackets
and black caps . . .
　a bit like sunflowers
nodding at the fence.

. . .*someone may have thrown*
　stolen money into your yard,
may we come in
　to look around?
I called Brindle and
　took her to her pen.
It seems a young man had
　snatched the jar for tips
at a restaurant on the Square
　and last was seen,
jar in hand,
　running toward
our Brazos View fence.

Neither money (nor culprit)
　was found, but
the event did make one
　stop to think—
this small town,
　like any town
large or small,
　has its good and
bad; most folks follow
　the rules and get along
but always there are some
　who snatch and run, or
break the laws in other ways.

Comanche Peak Power

Tucked neatly
  out of sight
behind Comanche Peak,
  the twin reactors
of our nuclear plant.
  Thousands of
homes and businesses
  depend upon
this facility
  for power and light.

Now Luminant
  wants to double
(or more than double)
  the power
generated at
  its plant.
Four reactors
  instead of two,
drawing much more water
  from our lake.

As area residents
  we went to hear
about their plans—
  engineers,
hydrologists, environ-
  mentalists
got right
  to the point—
generating nuclear power
  requires lots of water.

. . . and lots of
  security;
it took half an hour
  (after their presentation)
admitting us to the
  plant; handprints,
electronic wands,
  and an air gate
for loosing and detecting
  possible explosives dust.

This man-made massif—
  in hard hats
and protective eyewear
  we probed its
bowels and scaled
  its heights;
yet higher still
  the great gray
domed silos
  loomed.

Squaw Creek reservoir
  lay at our feet (its waters
cool the current reactors);
  the land green and
lush leading off
  toward the Peak—
buzzards soaring
  high above all,
effortlessly rising on
  the sun-warmed wind.

The Opposite Shore

Our immediate
  neighbors
show no lakeside
  lights, and
we show but few;
  yet the opposite
shore at night
  is aglow—
the commerciality
  of our lives—
Beall's, Lowe's,
  Wal-Mart, Home
Depot, and the
  fast foods,
branch banks and
  convenience stores
whose names we all
  know . . . their
neon signs and
  parking lot lights,
lining the bypass lanes,
  project distinctive
colors in wavering lines
  onto the dark waters
of the lake.

Pretty? Yes;
  illuminating
the practicalities
  of our times, but
quite an intrusion, too.
  Somehow I'd formed
the notion
  night was meant
to be stars, clear,
  air, clean,
moon pristine—
  most unlike the
aura of that far-side
  scene.
One might imagine
  how it must have
been, before the
  bypass was in—
a night-lit, slumbrous
  pasture field
within a loop
  of the slow river's
bend . . . no lights
  anywhere
to be seen.

Contrapuntal

Realms

Yesterday, a moth
   flailing with its wings
     at the window glass of
   the old toolshed, loosed scales like
dust from the chitinous structure of its
   wings: dooming itself to helplessness
     and prey. Not four feet away (in
   shadow) the toolshed door stood
ajar . . . but the insect was
   fixed on light. Its plight, in some
     respects, seeming similar to our own;
   by ancient patterns we struggle
to find our ways, as the moth in
   its set pattern took aim on light:
     and open doors near at hand,
   simply are beyond
our realms of sight.

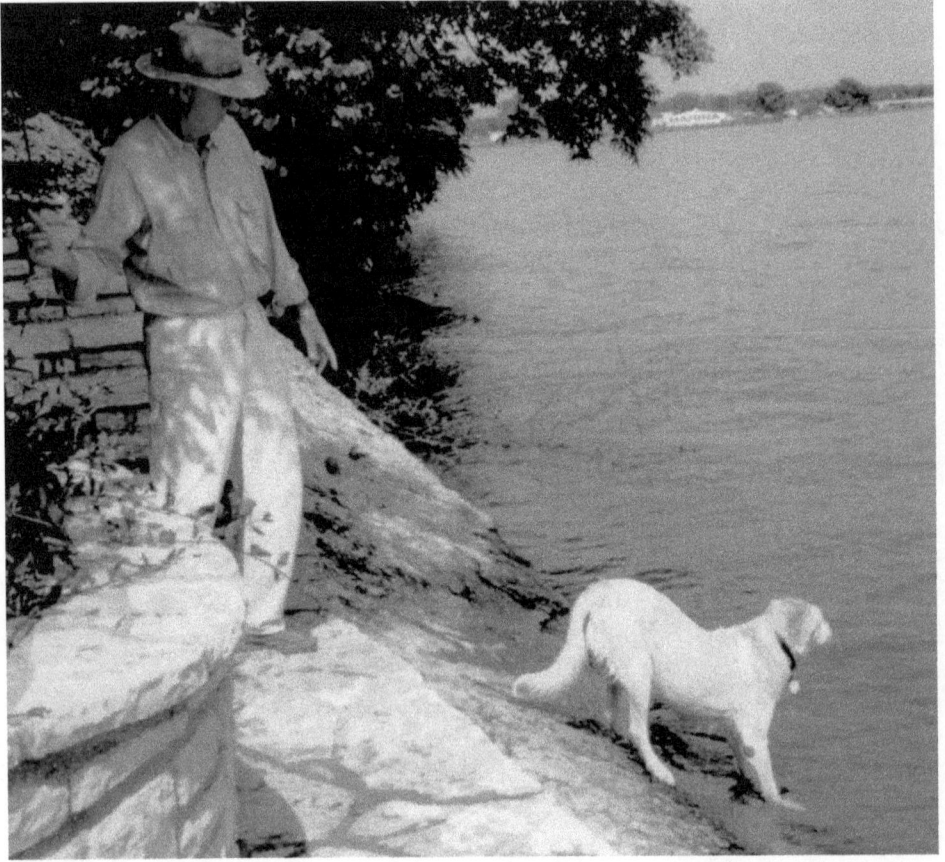

At Water's Edge

At Water's Edge

The rocks are
  mossy at
water's edge,
  great limestone
boulders turned
  on end, fallen
from the bluff, time
  knows when.

The wind blows,
  boats pass by,
waves lap against
  the bulwark forms,
then fall back
  to come again,
and again . . .
  unceasingly.

This is the place
  where Brindle swims,
year-round, late afternoons,
  launching her tawny
body into the waves
  for the *fetch*
I've thrown, which
  she retrieves.

Poets Laureate Tree

We have guessed
  the great live oak
shading the pergola
  and its terrace
to be about as old
  as the stone chimney
there, and its vast
  rooting nearly as old
as the well.

It tilts slightly north
  away from the bluff,
either rocks underneath
  shifted early on
or it's backing off
  from prevailing winds;
its thousands of acorns
  rain down
in the fall.

Here is where the double-
  hammock swings—
for looking up
  into the trees
for birds, or at night
  listening out for
the owls
  to conspire
with the breeze.

Cookouts,
  dinners,
book club meetings,
  rosarians
and garden classes,
  weddings (two),
and *Open Garden*
  for the town's Christmas
candlelight tours.

This great tree
  brooding over
it all—including,
  five years now,
Texas' poets laureate
  coming to read at
a lawn picnic event,
  a feature of an annual
arts review.

Langdon Review of the Arts
  In Texas, sponsored by
Tarleton University nearby—
  fiction, nonfiction,
painting, music, movies,
  and poetry; the
readings here so popular
  we have named this
tree, *Poets Laureate Tree*.

Offstage

The redbud
   at the edge
of our courtyard here,
   some leaves yellow,
some leaves green,
   seems just about ready
for a change of scene.

Winter Bypass

The moon
   hangs low
in our net
   of trees,
the lake
   a perfect
mirror of black,
   and jeweled light.

The night air
   crisp and quiet
here, while
   across the way
the bypass traffic
   sighs and rumbles,
east and west,
   rushing, both ways.

Christmas Songs

At winter solstice
   the year
is gathering in
   and Christmastime
is near, with
   holiday lights
strung along the
   fences here.

The large cedar
   beside the pergola
is festooned with lights
   and the pergola itself
with lights and bows
   adorned—
another Christmas season
   has come to Brazos View.

Our gardens were open
   for the Candlelight Tour
this year and several
   hundred people came,
the terrace fireplace
   warm and bright
as the choir from
   Happy Hill Farm sang.

Contrapuntal

A gentle
   morning hymn,
the early breeze
   brisk and clean
softly sighing in the
   cedar elm trees.

Perfect counterpoint
   in time and tone
to the clear, soft
   timbre
of the wind chimes
   hanging near.

The sun not quite
   over the rim,
the lake
   a metallic blue
with wind patterns
   shimmering.

The lower sky
   pale peach,
a pale paring
   of moon,
the morning star
   shining there.

Can Brazos View
   be any more than
counterpoint to what
   lies beyond—
this morning questions,
   the wind responds.

Two Chairs

Two chairs on
   an old front porch,
two chairs
   at the river's edge,
two chairs
   at roadside places
here and there,
   or our two chairs
at bluffside here,
   it's two chairs
side by side,
   everywhere.

What a fuss
   we make about life,
trying to get it
   figured out—
where to stand
   where to sit,
trying to get
   at the nub of it—
and those two chairs
   just sitting there,
so plainly show
   what it's all about.

Two Chairs

Breathe Deep

A spring shower
  has just passed,
Brazos View is
  fragrant and pristine;
earth and air
  smell fresh and clean.

Purple irises stand tall
  in an oaken bucket
placed lakeside,
  the kingfisher,
chattering
  as it rushes by
just beyond our dock.

A turtle is
  up for air,
a pair of sparrows
  gathers nesting grass;
Brindle and I
  stand, watch,
and breathe deep.

Night Sounds

The night sounds
  of Brazos View
we most like
  to recall:
wind impatient in
  our summer trees,
waves pushing
  against the shore,
farm dogs at a distance
  (left too long alone),
a late night train
  rolling in,
its attenuated call
  coming off
the prairie beyond
  the edge of town;
our owls answering back,
  and the crickets chirr, as
the muffled tower clock
  resolves it all—
the end of
  another day
at Brazos View.

A Poem for Later

Cetacean, the
  point at which
I will rest
  climbing up
the great stone stair . . .
  Brindle waiting
patiently, a step
  or two ahead,
to finish out
  the walk
which on this day,
  as on the many
days before,
  will have been an
activity we both
  looked forward to
with joy.

Brazos House Pergola

Charles Inge, a native Texan, lives with his wife, Dominique, on a rocky bluff overlooking the Brazos River's Lake Granbury.

Inge's earlier years were spent as a business executive in Dallas. Inspired by the lives and works of poets such as Wallace Stevens and William Carlos Williams, he reserved evenings and weekends for working at the craft of poetry.

Over time, travels to Europe and the Near East, writers' conferences, and completion of a Master of Liberal Arts degree at Southern Methodist University furthered his interest in writing.

He finds the compression, the immediacy, and intensity of poetry compelling. "An event, person, scene, feeling, or theme," Inge says, "can be developed and resolved on a single page. Poetry is the ideal genre for reading and writing in our busy, busy age."

www.ingramcontent.com/pod-product-compliance
Lightning Source LLC
Chambersburg PA
CBHW021109090426
42738CB00006B/569